"HELLO, GOD."

A PROCESS IN 3 STEPS

An Inspirational True Story and Practical Application
for Anyone Desiring a Faith-conscious Journey

SADA BELTRAN

"HELLO, GOD."

A Process in 3 Steps

ISBN-13: 9780692779705

Editor: Lisa Cerasoli, www.529Books.com
Interior Design: Danielle Canfield, www.529Books.com
Cover: Marie Bond, www.529Books.com

I dedicate this book to our family angel, Marie; my hero, Dominic; my mother, Rita; and to my awesome children and grandchildren. You are all Loved.

I would like to thank the Atlanta Bread Company in Summerville, South Carolina for allowing me to sit for hours, while writing this book in their wonderful establishment.

To fall in love with God is the greatest romance;

To seek Him the greatest adventure;

To find Him, the greatest human achievement.

—St. Augustine

Introduction

God whispered....and my life changed.

I wrote this book to share a message that came from God during one of the most anguishing times of my life. I believe with all my being, God gifted me with a way out, and it began when I heard His whispered guidance: *"Say Hello to Me through people and not their story."* Maybe this sounds like a parable, or just confusing to you, but that guidance birthed *"Hello, God."* You see, God is in all of us. His suggestion of saying hello to everyone—despite their background or belief system, regardless of where they came from, no matter where they were headed—this changed me.

This book is a detailed account of how God's Guidance delivered me back Home to Him. It's about the journey, the lessons, and the insights I gained along the way. The application of *"Hello, God:" A Process in 3 Steps* has been life-changing. Saying out loud, or even thinking the phrase, "Hello, God," has enabled me to greet God not just as my Higher Power, but as my friend every single time. I feel welcomed by God, and free to communicate directly and honestly with Him throughout the day now. I want to share my journey and my joy. This is my gift to you. I hope you enjoy it.

This process can be used by anyone who desires a closer walk with his or her Higher Power. The application of this process knows no distinction in faiths or beliefs; it matters not what you call your Higher Power, whether it be God, the Almighty, or Source, which are among some of the designations I've used in this book.

"HeLLO, GOD."
A PROCESS IN 3 STEPS

Part I:

Say Hello to God

Since you cannot do good to all,
You are to pay special attention to those
Who, by the accidents of time, or place, or circumstances,
Are brought into closer connection with you.

—St. Augustine

1

———— ·ℐℯ· ————

My Story

I FELT COMPELLED TO SHARE *"Hello, God:" A Process in 3 Steps* with others. I only intended to share about the process and very little about me and my story in this life. When I started this process, I tended to be reserved and cautious about what I shared with others. Living my "Hello, God" journey changed that. I found myself willing to be defenseless before God. After all, I'd laid my vulnerabilities bare before the Infinite and He loved me as He had always loved me. Now, I see God in everyone and anything.

I remember being as young as three years old believing in God and knowing He watched over me. I wouldn't call myself a religious person, but spiritual. I've read a lot of books, including the *New Testament, A Course in Miracles,* various books on Native American philosophies, and many others to arrive at answers about my faith. Yet, living my beliefs took time, and it was a while before I reached the true Peace of God.

They say times of struggle test us. Yet, God's peace can be found on the other side. My story begins during a time of struggle that eventually brought about the first time I achieved God's peace. I was struggling with leaving a safe career and steady income of twenty years, and so I prayed and prayed for a year, and I found genuine peace in 2003—and held onto that until 2011. But then, due to my own self-involvement, I slipped away from God. This is the story about my journey back.

It all started when I was preparing to retire from the military, after more than twenty years of service. My retirement date was set for the end of December 2002. I was stationed in Texas at the time. My son, Jerad, and I had lived there for eight years; it was the longest we had lived anywhere. Of all the places I've been stationed in the United States, Texas was my favorite. Retiring was not a decision I'd made lightly. I was taking a leap of faith.

Preparing for that departure was overwhelming. I had chosen to stay in the military for as long as I had because I liked the structure and the financial security it provided. Military living has its distinctions. I'd be leaving a shared camaraderie that would be absent in the future. The rank structure of management and knowing what responsibilities were expected of me would be gone. A whole way of living, that although challenging, I understood.

The scariest thought was leaping into a civilian job that did not guarantee a pay check every two weeks. My greatest fears in life have always revolved around money, and this move most definitely triggered that.

My work search landed me a job in Virginia; it had the best long term possibilities, but it was over a thousand miles away from Texas. When I'd originally made the decision to leave the military, Jerad was supposed to move with me. I was a single parent and Jerad and I were very close; it had always been just us. Jerad was eighteen and newly graduated from high school. His closest friends lived in Texas, and he especially didn't want to leave his high school love, Marie. When we found out he was going to be a father there was no way Jerad would leave his baby. He'd grown up without his father and would not let that happen to his child. I totally understood and supported him. Still, the thought of leaving my son behind hurt, and I ached to be there for him and his new family.

I was raised in a very traditional Mexican family where discipline was a way of life. Respect for elders and others was a must, and a very deep love of family came naturally. Unfortunately, no other family was nearby to help Jerad navigate being on his own for the first time. I was, however, blessed with some wonderful friends who offered to help him.

When the time came to retire and leave Jerad, I cried and cried. But, we needed a steady income. I was helping him financially to get started on his new life, and we had to get ready for the new baby boy who would be joining the family in July of 2003.

I went to see my mom who lived in Kansas before taking off to Virginia. I'm pretty close to my mom; my father had passed away in 1990. Most of my thirteen siblings lived in or around Kansas. We've always gotten along well. We have fun, rowdy get-togethers. The

3

stopover was a salve to my troubled spirit. This move was taking me away, yet again, from all of them.

After I left my mom and started the drive for Virginia, I kept questioning if I had made the right decision. Was Jerad going to be okay on his own? Maybe after the baby was born he and his new family could come live with me…? So, many unanswered questions.

I arrived in Virginia around the first part of January 2003. Before arriving, I found out that I had several friends who were stationed there. My friend, Faith, took me in for a couple of months. Despite Faith and knowing other military friends were there, I plummeted even further emotionally and spiritually. I felt guilty abandoning Jerad, and was stressing about making ends meet.

It was so disorienting living this whole new life away from my son, the military, work I understood, and I was missing family and friends. I had a hard time making sense of this new way of living. Faith has always been a resourceful woman, which was great because I was immobilized with hesitation and doubt. I didn't want to commit to staying, but knew I had to. I was looking for a place to live and not having any luck. It was Faith who found me a wonderful condo to rent. I loved it. It had a view of the river that helped soothe my troubled soul.

Through this whole period of adjustment, I prayed and prayed for peace and forgiveness. I begged God to help me weather through. I prayed for forgiveness in leaving Jerad and his future son.

I was spending most of my personal time alone. I've always been comfortable and confident doing things by myself; I enjoy my own company. However, now I was spending too much time in my head, thinking the same thoughts of whether to stay or go back to Texas or Kansas. I just couldn't commit to the job or life I had chosen. I missed Jerad and my family.

Faith had lent me some furniture (I had furniture in storage, but didn't send for it). I would sit at the table or on the floor looking out at the river. I meditated, beseeched, and prayed for the way forward. With all this alone time, I did a lot of self-reflection and looking back on my life. I faced-up to the many times I had caused hurt to others. I asked God for forgiveness. By the way, I believe God loves unconditionally, so the forgiveness I asked for wasn't really from God. He never held my mistakes against me; I did. I learned to forgive myself for my mistakes and the wrongs I had done to others. It was liberating to let go of all that guilt. I felt a clearing inside myself that soon would be replaced with God's peace.

I also prayed for someone, for something to help me move on and accept this new life. Answered prayer came in the form of Faith's wise and spiritual mother, Aleta. We became friends and she helped me see that being a recluse was not helping me get out of this funk. She gave me the push I needed to start living life where I was. I ventured out and started making friends and seeing the area.

My new friends and I shared similar spiritual beliefs and we would meet to talk, and just do things together. One of these friends told me about a book, *A Course in Miracles (ACIM)* that she found challenging to get through, but asked if I'd like to have it. I began reading *ACIM* and it touched me deeply. This book, along with daily mediation, brought me to the peace I'd been searching for.

It was a peace that permeated my being. In this state, I saw life with different eyes and understood my worldly concerns didn't have to identify me. I understood that I had obligations, but no longer felt the heavy weight of them. I was able to stand in observance of my world, rather than be caught in the drama of living it. I've never been one to hold many opinions or judgments, because I could often see the different sides of issues. I usually stepped away from these types of discussions, rather than getting drawn into them. In peace, I truly had no desire to be brought into discussions of how bad the world was going, not when I held God's love and peace in my being.

I'd always been one to live within myself and now, in peace, God kept company with me. God became more real than the world around me.

Jerad was never far from my thoughts. He was struggling at building his new life. We called each other often, and I flew back to see him when I could. Jerad called me one day distraught. This was before his son was born. It was a scary phone call from a heartbroken son to a mom so far away. I began to pray and meditate. I felt Spirit fill me and was given a prayer I use to this day: *I put in you God's Mind; you're safer there than you are in mine.* Amazingly, within a half hour, Jerad called back. He'd calmed down and worked out a way to deal with what had been troubling him. The power of faith. Not long after that, Jerad's son, Adrian, was born. I just missed his birth. What a chubby little guy he was when I did finally get him in my arms. He was perfect.

By this time my finances were in order. I was making more than enough to take care of myself and help Jerad and his family. I'd settled into a routine and began enjoying my life, but I missed my son and wanted to get to know my grandson. Jerad and his family drove out to Virginia during the winter months of 2004 to see if they could make a go of it. They stayed with me for a couple of months. It was wonderful having Jerad and company. My grandson, Adrian, was adorable, of course.

Jerad found work and Marie stayed home to take care of Adrian. Marie had never been away from home, and eventually she and Adrian flew back. It was such a sad time. Jerad and Marie weren't sure their relationship was going to last. Jerad stayed behind with me and worked, but he couldn't stand being away from Adrian and drove back a few months later.

Meanwhile, my new job required frequent travel between Virginia and Massachusetts. Through the course of these travels, I met Dominic, who was destined to be my husband. I remember the first time I met him. He was working on some PowerPoint slides that were to be presented to upper management. I noticed a few errors and suggested some corrections. The quiet me could kindly, but firmly do this sort of thing. I didn't know at the time that Dominic was not someone most people corrected. People in the office were surprised when he actually made the changes.

After that, I became the one everyone sent to tell Dominic about things that needed attention. We became good work partners and did a lot of traveling together, not just back and forth between those two areas, but also to other place across the United States. Eventually, our relationship evolved into a courtship. Dominic was God's answer to a prayer I had written a while back, asking for a mate—asking that "our love for each other be a reflection of God's love for us." Dominic is a good, ethical, and honest man. He has strong spiritual convictions and told me he was drawn to my peacefulness.

I cherished my peace and would not allow anyone or any circumstances in my space that could hinder it. Though I cared deeply for Dominic, there came a time when his unfairly harsh treatment of a coworker disturbed me. I calmly let him know that I would not allow this in my space. He remedied the situation by apologizing to the individual. His actions demonstrated that he was sincere, not only about loving me, but also that he valued my peace and was working to find it for himself.

We both had to get jobs in the same area to be together, and two opened up in Washington DC. In April of 2005 we flew to Kansas (for a "supposed" surprise birthday party for me). We even flew in Jerad and Adrian from Texas. Dominic shocked my mom and the rest of my family by asking for my hand in marriage. It seemed that my family thought of me as the runaway bride. After the shock wore off, they all embraced him into the family.

We set a wedding date for October of that year to be married in my Kansas hometown. My loving, giving mother took care of all the wedding details; she outdid herself. Mom and Jerad walked me down the aisle. After the ceremony, a horse-drawn, pumpkin-shaped carriage (that mom had leased), took us from the church to the reception.

Jerad and Dominic, by this time, had established the foundation for a father and son relationship. And, so we became a blended family—Dominic with his daughter, Kay and future husband, Richard; Jerad, his wife Marie, and two-year-old Adrian. Thankfully, Jerad and Marie had worked through their issues.

We returned to DC and were living a happy, peaceful, spiritual life together, and we were building our financial future by investing in properties in my beloved Texas. I traveled often to see Jerad and his family.

Kay had also been in the military and decided to leave after six years and found work in DC. It was a wonderful time for Dominic and me to have Kay move in with us for a short period. It gave us a chance to get to know each other. I was deeply honored that Kay shared her confidences with me. It was the beginning of what grew into a true mother and daughter relationship.

Kay's fiancé, Rick, who was still in the military, received orders to move to Illinois and they chose to have a quiet ceremony with just the two of them. They have blessed us with two granddaughters, Kayla and Izzy.

Dominic and I both enjoy small-town living and decided we'd like to move to a more intimate community. The synchronicity of prayer is amazing. Dominic was offered a telecommuting job that allowed us to move to a quiet little town in Texas in the fall of 2007. One of our Texas properties, a house near the lake, hadn't sold yet, and we were able to move in. Dominic started working from home and traveling to San Antonio, where his main office was, when necessary.

When we made this move we knew that it wasn't likely that I would find the type of work I had been doing. We had been doing well financially, and were prepared for that. So, I went about getting our new house in order. I wasn't used to not working. That was a real shift for me.

Dominic and I both tended towards being introverts. We met our neighbors, but maintained a certain distance. To help me transition from not working, I started routine walking and volunteering for the local family crisis center that offered services for victims of domestic violence (DV) and sexual assault (SA).

My life was everything I'd prayed for and more. I had a stable, wonderful, loving relationship, a beautiful house, we were settling into our small community, and we had a new addition to the family—a cute little white Shih Tzu dog, Dino. And, as a wonderful added bonus, Jerad and his family only lived a short distance away. On top of that, mom and my siblings were a day's drive, instead of having to board a plane to visit.

I looked for work but wasn't having luck finding it in my previous field as an analyst or trainer. It's amazing how opportunities fall into our laps when we're in synch with our faith. The shelter I had been volunteering at had an opening for a DV and SA peer counselor, and I applied. I was chosen and started in August of 2008. I thought I was pretty much on the right path and gave thanks for answered prayers and God's peace.

I was living a beautiful, rewarding life. I found my work challenging and intensely gratifying. This is the type of work I'd dreamed of doing, helping others. It was ideal for me. I was able to offer a listening ear and help people work through their issues and concerns. Friends, family, and co-workers all told me this was my calling. And there it was. When Infinite's child is ready the door opens.

This played to many of my strengths. I had background in this work, but I wanted to be so much better. I researched and went to seminars to expand my knowledge. I'm a reader; books have been a constant resource for inspiration and answers.

As a child I would go to the library and check out a dozen books at a time for the two-week period. My nose was either in a book, helping mom with the house and kids, or outside playing. Things would go on around me, family stuff here and there, and I'd ask how come no one told me. I'd been so caught up in reading I hadn't heard what was happening around me.

Dominic and I had been doing spiritual reading together; but that would come and go in waves. The soul, like the body, needs to be nurtured daily to stay healthy. Gradually day-to-day living began taking up more and more of our time. My work was engrossing me, which wouldn't have been a bad thing if I'd relied on God to guide my path, but I had started relying on me. Dominic attempted to point out that I was carrying my work home. I didn't see it.

By this time the economic crisis of 2008 was impacting us. Our house still hadn't had a reasonable offer, and we had another property (in addition to the lake house) that wasn't selling either. Dominic's work was running into roadblocks and we were concerned about how long he'd have a job. He was working on contracts that kept him employed for months at time, but previously it had been years. In 2011, his work became chancier. That's when we informed our realtor that we might need to consider ways to turn over our house.

Fortunately, in the knick of time, Dominic's company had an opening on a temporary contract in South Carolina.

Dominic left to work there in May.

Dino and I were on our own. Normally, this would not have bothered me; I was used to being by myself. However, this time I felt isolated. We lived in an area with mostly weekenders for neighbors. Even if I only spoke occasionally to them, I found comfort in having others close by, just in case. I also knew of a woman who had been raped in a town near us, and I found myself getting scared—double checking the locks, closing the blinds and curtains, and even kept a bat near my bed. You'd think at this point my declining reliance on God should have been evident to me. If only I'd been paying attention.

I compare my spiritual crisis to driving down the road and having a pebble hit the windshield. One pebble is fine. It's a nick. But more kept coming. The windshield held strong. It looked fine. I could still see out of it. But the nicks and pings kept coming. One day the window just shatters. That was me. I was starting to crack. Eventually I shattered.

I was worrying about how we would make it if Dominic lost his job. These thoughts weighted heavily on my mind. Money triggers from childhood came back full blown. I think my fear is rooted in watching and listening to my parents struggle and work hard to take care of all fourteen of us. Those were not easy times; we grew up in a small town where discrimination was the norm. I internalized my fear and carried it into adulthood. I have a saying: *There are many surprises in life; be picky.* This means roll with life as it happens. But, money was the one area that I felt the pressure of *now*—whatever involved debt had to be paid *now*. I knew logically this was not realistic, but it would get the best of me.

The next ping began with work. As a peer counselor, I would listen to women recount tragic stories of how they had been beaten and sometimes raped. I'd work with them on how to cope and incorporate new life skills. But after three years, the healthy boundaries I had established started failing me. I had a session with a new client who had been raped. She numbly recounted the night. I listened with an open heart and just let her talk. We met several times. Her story keenly impacted me. It was hard to put it aside. I had entered into her nightmare. That is never good for a counselor. A few days later, another client came in and she had also been raped. I wasn't able to separate myself and ended up internalizing their horrors. It became difficult for me to sit through a session after that. I became hypersensitive to sexual matters; something as small as what someone would wear could set me on edge.

Overwhelming apprehensions developed—they were loaded with confusion and anguish. I didn't gradually go into burnout; I was okay one day and then the next—the car window shattered.

I thought before this happened that I had a great deal of compassion for my clients' suffering; but after conquering my own mental and spiritual torments, I have far greater appreciation, and more empathy, for the struggles they go through to get to the other side of mental clarity. Please let me say I in no way can fully comprehend the depths of their pain; their sufferings didn't happen to me. My heart goes out to all survivors.

Money anxieties, fear of physical harm and rape, missing Dominic—it kept building, one anxiety on top of the other. These dreads plagued me daily and into the night.

Why didn't I reach out for help?

I thought I could handle it.

I'd always managed to get through life's other curveballs. I'm the one others turn to, not the other way around. I foolishly duped myself into thinking I was coping. I was applying life tools to help myself deal with my racing thoughts, wasn't I? My goodness, I should have been able to, I taught them to others. Hadn't I instructed clients? *You need to share, write it down, do affirmations, be positive, etc....* My pride kept me from reaching out for help; that was my job—to have the answers. I didn't want to be viewed as weak, or be a burden. Talk about not taking my own advice. I even let myself believe I had gotten a foothold on things. The thin fabric of my faith was not strong enough to maneuver through what was unfolding.

Then more change: Dominic was told that if he wanted to keep his job he'd need to move to South Carolina permanently. We had to move. We had hoped to stay in Texas and settle down, instead of moving every four years. But first, if any of this were to happen, we had to get a reasonable offer on the house. It finally came in September of 2011. Hallelujah! We were sincerely grateful.

The closing was in October. Dominic couldn't come back, so packing the two-story house was a task I took on. This triggered my fibromyalgia, an autoimmune disease that causes nerve ending pain and exhaustion. My son came to help as much as he could, as did a wonderful friend. That was a welcome relief.

Fortunately, one of our neighbors knew of a cute little house I could move into temporarily, but it wasn't suitable for Dino. I had to send the little guy to stay with Jerad. My little buddy, my faithful companion, was gone.

Meanwhile, Dominic and I planned out that I'd move after Thanksgiving. The plan was more about me saying goodbye to some close friends before meeting up at my mother's for Christmas. From there, we would travel back to Texas—to load our household furnishings that were in storage, say goodbye to mutual friends in our community, see Jerad and company, pickup Dino, and make our way to South Carolina.

I gave notice at work. Even with the burnout going, this meant leaving a profession I'd come to cherish. I was leaving clients who had shared some of their deepest confidences and relied on me to help them. There was parting with treasured friends, and Jerad and his family. It also meant moving further away from my mom and other family members. As I said, I'm pretty close to my mom. Just knowing she was a few hours away had been a comfort.

Throughout this time I deceived myself into thinking I'd get it together once Dominic and I could talk things over and life would eventually even out. I'd always dealt with life and its issues by myself. I'd rarely turned to anyone to share deep confidences or ask for guidance. I was used to shouldering my life until Dominic came along and he became my best friend. I needed him.

I started my trip thinking it would give me time to work through everything. I remember driving and hoping, beseeching and praying to be delivered from this purgatory I existed in.

How could someone who had been living the dream get to this point?

I simply had this feeling of doom and I could not shake it. I couldn't get out of my head, thoughts of being hurt, of being poor, of being "whatever" just wouldn't stop. I needed someone to confide in; I needed to let God in, but kept getting in my own way.

My first stop was to see a cherished friend in upper Texas; then onto New Mexico to visit two friends, one a longtime confidante and a much-loved peer counselor I had worked with. After that I made a stop in Colorado to see one of my sisters. I finally arrived at Mom's in Kansas. Her care and love was a maternal balm to my disturbed heart. I didn't tell mom anything. I don't like to worry her. Just feeling her love made a difference.

At long last Dominic arrived. I used to tell my DV group I wished he could come for show and tell; he's such an incredible partner. I had missed his reassuring presence.

Reflecting back, I can see the subtle, gradual twists and turns that programmed the course that set me adrift. My thoughts had gone astray, and I relied less and less on God, and more on the world outside me.

I came to understand that I'd taken God for granted. I had slumbered in the comfort of knowing God, and had stopped working at my relationship with my Source. I know now that it was my ego that led me to think I was dealing with life issues. By the time I acknowledged I had slipped out of the peace of God's love, the cancer of ego had eaten away at my faith.

Dominic and I finally made it to South Carolina in Jan 2012. I summoned up the nerve to tell him about how much turmoil I had been experiencing, and still was, since he'd been gone. He listened, letting me get it all out, then he held me in total acceptance, wishing I had talked to him sooner. But he would have rushed home, and I had been determined not to burden him. It felt so good to be held and cradled in his loving, comforting embrace. He reassured me of his love, his commitment to us, and gave me the space and time to begin working my way through the grueling maze of my qualms, fears, and dreads.

I was finally in a safe environment, and I hobbled my way toward miniscule successes.

The safety of being with Dominic helped me begin establishing a daily routine, which I knew was essential at this time. I'd been spending too much time in the house and it was wearing on me. Dino and I explored our new neighborhood.

The next thing I worked on was building a support system and adding activities, so as not to rely so much on Dominic. I felt the need to integrate into this new city, so I looked for places to volunteer, but there were paperwork delays. Waiting, waiting—I really wanted to get back into the groove of purposeful living. I wanted to get back to work and applied for multiple jobs.

I worked at getting settled in by using the tools I'd taught to others. I started phoning and sharing just a little with some long distant friends, using positive affirmations, visualizations, walking Dino, meditating with, and on, God daily. I went by myself for walks, biked, and even did some running. I couldn't find enduring peace. It eluded me. I literally ached for quiet to silence the chatter of my mind so I could hear God's Holy Spirit guidance.

I clearly recall the moment peace arrived. It was an early, crisp spring morning in late March of 2012. I was (once again) attempting to get quiet during meditation. In one small space, for just a moment—I must have let go enough—and God's inspiration revealed itself. I had slipped into my favorite visualization spot, where I would see myself calmly sitting under an ancient, fully bloomed, shady tree atop a grassy knoll. I could even feel the wind gently blowing through the leaves and the silky ankle-length grassy field that spread out all around me under my legs, softening my seat on the ground. Above me was a translucent blue sky with spattering wisps of white clouds. Sitting under the tree, I heard God whisper: *"Say hello to Me through people and not their story."*

I sat there with tears trickling down my face, experiencing feelings of peace, of God's love for me. My heart knew release was possible now. I felt as though I was being washed ashore to safety. I felt encircled and infused with a profound glowing peace. I lingered in this space with God feeling so very, very thankful.

I had heard God. He had guided me to start saying hi to everyone in the world around me because it meant I was saying hello to Him. And that's what was going to save me—developing a close friendship with God.

And now my life is a miracle of change.

2

The Answer and Solution

IF GOD'S GUIDANCE ISN'T CLEAR to you right now, it's okay. I promise it will become evident as you read on. In short for now, God was guiding the introvert in me to say hello directly to Him through His children. When I was a kid I was called shy. I used to be cautious of making the first move, of saying hi to anyone, stranger or acquaintance. As an adult, I'd been labeled quiet, an introvert. Saying "hi" randomly for me required courage. I mean, I had to take into account whether someone would say "hi" back. Or maybe I didn't particularly like the way that person looked; maybe they looked angry, or maybe, if already knew them, I didn't agree with their opinions. Bottom line—I used to come up with excuses to stay distanced. What I began to understand, though, was that I was judging people by their appearance, by their outlook…*by their stories*. And that should not matter. God was in them, that was what was IMPORTANT. That's all that really mattered. Not their story.

God's insight: *"Say Hello to Me through people and not their story,"* also provided the solution on how to make this a working refrain in my life, say "Hello, God." I was excited! I was going to do this.

It is my conviction that God is unconditional love. This is the foundation of my belief, even though I had strayed away.

God graced me with this "hello" inspiration to help me find my way back. However, I ran into a slight hiccup. How was I to go about saying "Hello, God" when this was not my norm? I did recognize this greeting wasn't about me, it wasn't about what someone might think of me, or even the impressions I'd get from them.

You might be thinking, "Can't she just pray?" or, "It's just 'hello' for goodness' sake." Yes, I could continue to talk to my Source in thankful prayer or beseeching need, but this was a very different way to address God. I was *intentionally* conveying God into my "hello." This was no longer a casual greeting. This hello was purposely being directed to God. So, I mulled it over, and lo and behold a pretty simple process unfolded:

1. Focus on the person being addressed.

2. Direct attention to the middle of the person's forehead; that's the "hello" spot. (After some practice, you'll likely end up looking directly at the person's face.)

3. Say "hello" and think of God as you address that person. This is God we're addressing. Make the most of it!

The solution was so simple. Drumroll please…I could do this! I now had a simple process to "see" God in every person. I decided to start the hellos on my daily walks with Dino because he was an extremely sociable little guy.

Wow! Could it really be that simple? After all, the inspiration and the solution had come from God. I couldn't go wrong. God's clarity had come to me in those few moments of quiet and I was on my way Home. I kept thanking God for the simplicity of the solution. By the way, I use this word "Home" often as a way to express being and living God, rather than heaven.

Although the process sounded simple, it would take time and lots of practice to change *my thought process*, to make this second nature. Let me explain how I started.

Step 1
Focus on the person being addressed.

I have to admit when I thought about just focusing on someone, it did feel a little weird at first. I was used to doing a *hit and run* hello, and now I was acknowledging with God intent. This played with my head. Before saying the first hello, I practiced visualizing myself offering a friendly God smile greeting. This gave me a chance to process through some of the awkward feelings of doing something different. *What if they ignore me?* That was a big fear. I reminded myself this was about seeing God in them, not about what I noticed, or (as I received from God) not about whatever their story was.

Here's how I started. Dino and I would go out for our walks and as someone would approach, a little conversation would go off in my head: *Okay, remember this is to God. Just look at the person.* So, that's what I did. Like I said, it felt a little weird to begin with, but I just kept taking the plunge and committed to focusing on the person. Does that sound a little funny—focusing? I did not normally focus on someone when I used to say "hi", my natural inclination had been: *Maybe I'll just walk on by, and if they say something, then I will.*

Depending on who you are this could be the easiest or hardest step. It depends on whether you find it easy to talk to others (my son can talk to almost anyone). Some people prefer to avoid talking, and then there are some who aren't sure whether to talk or not. (That used to be me.) Sometimes, we forget we're not the only ones going through these feelings. There are all kinds of people in this world. Not to worry; I found after many days of greetings, more often than not, others were looking for the opening to share a smile, but they weren't sure of how *I* would react to them. Even if someone doesn't respond, it's not a reason to stop. Remember this is about you meeting God through communication with them.

So, at any rate, I got past the first step.

Step 2
Address the middle of the forehead.

Addressing the middle of the forehead (what some call the third eye) took me, I felt, to the place where minds meet. The place where we share in the Mind of God, where we are One in God's balanced, beautiful, joyful, loving, serene mind. Regardless of our choices in this life, God's Mind is where we've originated from, and abide to-day. Even if we've lost our way, God still knows us. So, the joining of our individual minds can be a meeting place in God's Oneness. It doesn't get much better than that.

Also, by focusing on someone's forehead we are less likely to get distracted by their appearance, making it easier to take the leap and "see" God's presence. I've wondered if "seeing" God's light in someone is actually the geneses for artists to paint halos around their subject's heads—just a thought.

In a less spiritual light, addressing the middle of the forehead gives the impression that you are looking someone in the eye. I'm happy to report that directly addressing someone has become pretty much effortless. The responses I do or do not receive—good, bad, or indifferent—no longer hold significance, because more often than not I "see" God in others.

Step 3
Say "hello" and think of God as you address that person.

Here's the step where I actually say hello (out loud or silently) to someone—take the leap and be the first to say hi. At first, I had to remind myself that this is about acknowledging God in this person. Previously, my "hi" would have been a quick drive-by, and that was if I said anything at all. Sometimes, rather than looking at someone,

I would divert my eyes. That way I didn't have to know whether they responded or not.

Admittedly, I was uncomfortable at the beginning, but I persevered and didn't let uncomfortable feelings of embarrassment stop me. With my history of hesitation, I knew it would be a bit discombobulating; this was about going outside my comfort zone and stretching my wings.

This is why I've mapped out my user-friendly process—for those of you who may need it.

$$\infty$$

I had to make a conscious commitment to make this process in 3 steps work for me. Because thinking about doing something and actually doing it are two different matters. This was important, for I truly felt God had given me this process to help me make my way back Home. I committed myself to making this process work. I kept reiterating: *I'm talking to God through this person.* This made it easier to avoid the distraction of someone's appearance. This was the beginning of eliminating subjectivity—mine. It was the vehicle that let me get out of the way and "see" God in others.

Each new greeting uplifted me as I bonded with another through God. It wasn't sometimes, but every, single time. It was as though a luminous smile lit up my soul. With each "hello" I sensed the shedding of worries, and Infinite's Spirit light ratcheted up and up, till I felt a glowing inside. It's changed me.

Behind me were the stumbling, hollowed shadows, and ahead was the leisurely spiraling, soothing light of Source that literally saturated my being. I came to rest in God's iridescent, all-encompassing, compassionate love. Doesn't that sound like the perfect place call Home? Through God's love I was evolving and voyaging back Home, much like the prodigal son. Source was simply waiting for me to wake up, yet again.

In the beginning, cresting waves of skepticism and doubt would creep in. Obnoxious questions kept trying to intrude: *Do I really have the right to talk directly to God? Am I being overly courageous here? Am I being brazen to think I could actually just say, "Hello, God"? Am I tempting fate going directly to God?*

Yes, to some it might seem like I had a lot of nerve thinking little ol' me had the right to chat casually with God. And, yeah, it did feel almost sacrilegious—me, going directly to the Big Being without any type of intermediary, such as a pastor, priest, or anyone else who had dedicated their profession to being the go-between. I knew to some this would be considered stepping outside the doctrinal box to go straight to God without a ministry official to intercede on my behalf.

I have to admit the thought of addressing God directly did feel a little irreverent; it went against some of the creeds I'd grownup with. I wondered about being offensive. I wondered what people would think of me. Was I being brazen? Maybe I was, but I was going to do this, go straight to God's Essence—the spark of life in all human beings, in everything there is.

I would touch God's Essence in myself and others. I believe God's Essence is the total sum of love, total acceptance, and infinite joy. God's Essence is in each and every one of us. If this was being brazen it was worth it!

This process in 3 steps has allowed me to invoke (continually) my connection to God through the simple use of an unassuming, conventional greeting. It has re-established the connection I'd let slip away. This gesture strengthens and nourishes my God connection daily.

The application of this process in 3 steps ushered in a new frame of mind.

It's brought me Home.

3

Why Was This a New Way of Addressing God?

MOST OF US HAVE TURNED to God asking for blessings, or prayed and beseeched God to deliver us from difficult situations. After all, this is what I'd been doing. But asking for a blessing and saying hi to God are not the same.

Here are a few *Merriam Webster Dictionary* definitions to clarify.

Blessing—approval that allows or helps you to do something: help and approval from God: something that helps you or brings happiness.

I'd already asked for God's approval or help. This was something new. I was saying, "Hi, God," but through others, so this didn't fit.

Prayer—an address (as a petition) to God or in word or thought: a set order of words used in praying: an earnest request or wish.

I'd already prayed and been answered, I needed something that I could act on after answered prayer.

Beseeching—to beg (someone) for something: to ask (someone) in a serious and emotional way to do something.

I'd done a whole lot of beseeching, begging for help. God had answered my prayer and blessed me with saying: *"Say Hello to Me through people and not their story."* This had taken me to "hello."

Hello—an expression or gesture of greeting.

This use of "hello" became a statement that God is and that I am in God, (just as are you). It was an acknowledgement of fact— a "knowingness" that is unchangeable. God IS, and God IS in everyone.

"Hello" for me meant coming face-to-face, so to speak, with God through everyone and all things. It brought me to God's peace and love.

In saying hi to God, I didn't have to wait to know a story, or know anything personal about the person I was addressing. I share this because I'm an intuitive person. People will often open up to me with little prompting; this is an honor I don't take lightly. With this greeting, however, I didn't have to know them and this made it so easy for me to say hi to a total stranger. Whatever impressions came across didn't have to be the reason I either did or did not address someone.

"Hello, God" then became a people equalizer. It was impossible to think someone was better than me, or that I was better than someone. When I addressed God in them, who or what they were became less relevant. Talk about being humbled before God.... I began to grasp the actuality of what *true humility* is about. I experienced this humility again and again as I addressed God's children. I began to get an inkling of what standing in God's glory must feel like; it was breathtaking. It humbled me. My worldly woes began receding in the face of God's glory. *How could they not?* The world is not greater than God.

Perhaps someone reading this loves the idea of experiencing God in others and would love to stand in God's glory, but might have a second thought and think: What about the bad stuff people do? How can someone be treated as God's child when as mortals we do some terrible things to ourselves, each other, and this world? I bring this up because family and friends in the past have told me that I look at the world through rose-colored glasses, or that I'm too willing to give others the benefit of the doubt.

Yes, terrible things do happen in this life. But, what if we shifted our view and learned to see each other as God sees us? I believe that in God's eyes we are perfection. When we look through our Source's eye, the imperfections of this world no longer hold us captive.

Let me share an *aha moment* I had about twenty years ago that helped me begin to see the Light in others. I was home recovering from minor surgery to my foot. I was sitting in my burgundy recliner watching a daytime talk show. My right foot was elevated because it was in a cast. The guest was sharing about how to talk to the Christ in others, and in ourselves, and to use this as a way to reach out.

This idea of talking to Christ immediately appealed to the intro-vert in me, who steered clear of being the first to say hi or initiate conversation (but was comfortable talking and praying to God). This was the push I'd needed to reach out. After hearing this, I got into my car and drove into town. I went hobbling into several stores visualizing Christ in the center of people's bodies, and I actually started greeting them. It was so cool. I felt so happy and light-hearted. I recall one cashier looking at me a little funny. I wasn't sure if it was because I offered such a warm greeting and it made him feel good, or because he thought this woman with a cast on her foot was overly friendly and odd. After thirty years of averting eye contact, I was awkward—standing in the middle of the store, cast on my leg, shooting off greetings like I should have been wearing a blue nametag from Walmart. It helped me overcome some of my self-consciousness in talking to others, but I still wasn't wholly at ease. And neither were the recipients of my greetings. There was definitely going to be an adjustment period.

This second time around, after hearing God speak directly to me, I was determined not to let my relationship with the Infinite slip away. I was going to live in God daily by consciously feeling/seeing Him in others. I was *certain* that saying hello to God through others would unequivocally do the trick; after all it was His message, His gift to me. My part was to stick with it and follow through.

I originally viewed this particular quest to the Almighty Power as another tool in my spiritual toolbox, but in retrospect "*Hello, God*" wasn't just a tool for a new chapter in my life; it was a new beginning. It is an ongoing quest that has changed my day-to-day living in this world. This venture has taught me ways to dwell in God by letting go of my ego, judgments, and the prejudices that have so often handicapped me.

I'd love for you to share this experience of wondrous joy and peace. Living in the daily presence of God's love has allowed me to feel, perceive, see, sense, and talk to Him.

4

"Hello" A Simple Greeting

I AM WHOLLY CONVINCED THE idea to say hello to God's children was an inspiration from God. This became evident as my fears slowly abated each day. Connecting with God through this simple, happy greeting made me aware of something I had never taken note of: the many different ways there are to greet someone. My goodness there are so many—hi, hello, hey, how are you, how ya doin', good morning, good afternoon, good evening, and many more. I've used them all to bring both of us—me and the recipient—into the circle of the Almighty's love.

It colossally astounds me how the use of this simple greeting was the key to opening the door to God's peace. I just had to use it and then step through the entrance to be reconnected to God's love and peace.

Hello is such a simple act that most of us tend not to give it much thought, other than using it as a casual way to greet others. Yet, it's given me God. This sometimes offhanded, cursory gesture has been the tool that has allowed me to have a closer walk and friendship with God. Our new relationship has ushered in so many enlightenments. All this from a simple little courtesy that sometimes had escaped me.

This process in 3 steps that came about from a simple hello, has been recalibrated through God's grace, for a new purpose. It is now a way to connect and extend loving kindness and consideration, be it in a quick passing, while walking or running, in stores or wherever I am. I enjoy this new purpose behind all of my greetings. Each time I verbally or silently recognize another in God, I hope that person feels the same joy I experience.

When I go about recalling my days now, I get a warm fuzzy feeling. Each day I know that I've seen God in each person through my hellos and that, when possible, I took the time to ask someone about themselves. I truly enjoy talking with people. What I really find intriguing is that now the new people in my life and old friends think I'm extroverted. Now that's a switch. All this happiness from a small gesture that only takes a few moments out of my day.

This simple greeting: "Hello, God," opened up a new life path for me—one that I compare to pioneering across new territory, just like the settlers of old, that has been sun-kissed by God.

5

My First "Hello, God"

THIS WAS MY TICKET HOME. I knew in my soul this would work; I just had to get started. I was determined to follow through with God's message to me. I was so intent on making this work that I didn't dwell on being hesitant or nervous as I started out the next day on my walk with Dino. We stepped out the door into a lovely early spring afternoon. We lived in a well-established subdivision, where the homeowners took pride in maintaining their lawns, along with caring for a diversity of multi-colored flowering shade trees, towering pine trees, and a variety of shrubs. The sky was mostly clear with a few wisps of lazy white clouds. There was a slight breeze stirring the flowers and trees, and the temperature was mild.

The very first person I see is the grumpy-looking man who lived nearby. I'd seen him out working on his lawn regularly. He always looked like he didn't want to be bothered. He just gave off that vibe. I guess God has a sense of humor—that this man just happened to be the first person we came across. I mentally went through the process: focus, direct attention, say hello. Yes, I actually visualized saying hello to him. I felt God with me and so I worked up my courage.

"Hello," I said to the grumpy man.

He grudgingly acknowledged me.

I felt like running my hand across my forehead and saying "Whew." I'd done it. I think it went reasonably well. Best of all, I felt God to the very core of my being. It was an amazing *soul-deep* knowing of God. Can you imagine having a soul-deep connection like that all the time? The awe, the profound sense of gratitude had me feeling like a little kid dancing around in a sunlit spring rainfall. I felt God's joy and love so deeply—like when my dad was able to come to one of my school Christmas programs. This experience of God's delight in me, His child, was something else, kid-like feelings cropped up everywhere. God's love enfolded me and gave me the feeling of being in my parent's comforting, loving embrace, only way, way better.

I kept telling myself I addressed God! GOD! Me, I spoke directly to GOD!

Each greeting I have offered since is beguiling and sincere, and just like the very first hello, I smile inside from feeling God's eternal love is for me.

I went headlong into greeting everyone the rest of that walk. I did feel a bit funny and awkward that first day. I probably came across a bit strong because I was practicing at being comfortable with this new me and I was so happy saying hello, God.

"Hello, God" greetings transformed our ordinary walks into enchanting sessions of plugging straight into God's love. Each person has become an entryway to God's presence. Knock and the door will be open. "Hello" became my knock on the door, each person acted as the door or entranceway to God, and God always answered.

6

The Journey Began

SITTING HERE WRITING I MARVEL at the simplicity of this inspiration that evolved from an unpretentious "Hello, God." Much as the voilà wave of a magician's wand, "Hello, God" miraculously delivered me into Source's presence. A simple, harmless gesture steadily hand-over-hand hauled me out of my limbo. I was delivered onto the peaceful, calm shores of Infinite's Mind. I would repeat: *I am safe. At long last, I'm safe.*

Behind me I could see the path I'd walked that had, hopefully, completed lessons that I'd lived and learned from; if not completed, as least advanced. Teaching me, once again, peace comes through God.

Saying "Hello, God," has been the catalyst that launched a new way of living. Each greeting restored the light in my soul. Each gesture honored God in me, others, and the Almighty's creations. Each day's greetings transports me Home while here on earth, because I see God in all things.

The initial payoff of plugging into God was immediately and literally electrifying; it popped me out of my melancholy and misery. It's been over a year of growth and guidance. I remind myself daily—people are not their circumstances. I remind myself, this is God's child and that's all that matters. These reminders keep me from getting caught-up in their story, meaning the impressions I get before greeting them, or the judgements. All that matters is that I extend them God's unconditional love. Remembering this is important.

During the first month of my journey, I felt my troubled mind easing. My anxiety and avoidance of others decreased with each God greeting, and it was enough to keep me pushing forward. I would walk about two miles a day with Dino, and I'd get the biggest kick out of greeting people. What a change from my drive-by hellos (or from saying nothing at all). This was fast becoming the best part of my day.

I began to think: *I'm feeling like part of the neighborhood.* I was becoming part of belonging to something. That was significant for me. My world was starting to make sense. I got to know our next-door neighbor. She was the embodiment of southern hospitality and showed me around town. This was God at work.

I conscientiously worked at turning things over to God. The more I turned things over the sooner positive changes began to happen. I began getting calls backs on volunteering. I woke up ready to engage my day. On our walks I started noticing and enjoying the sunny days, instead of dwelling on my old fears. And thankfully, I began getting call backs on volunteering.

At month two, Dino and I met another friend while walking. She had two dogs, and she readily welcomed us into her world. This was the quickest I'd ever socialized with anyone in all my eleven moves. I got involved with a reading group. And of course, I was diligently greeting everyone I came across on walks with Dino. This provided me with a constant lift-up.

I was seeing God just about everywhere. I'd expanded my hellos to include nature. I'd look at leaves and say, "Hi, God," and it would almost bring me to tears knowing God was all around me. South Carolina is so scenic; it was easy to see Source.

Three months into this journey it dawned on me to write a book, but this idea was still just percolating in the back of my mind. I'd toyed with the idea of a book over the years. I'd even come up with several titles, but always talked myself out of it.

I started volunteering with an agency that dealt with domestic violence. My husband was concerned about my doing this type of work again, but I felt I was in the proper frame of mind to handle it. I'd been working hard at putting those troubling issues in God's Mind where they were safe, and with God's help they got resolved.

The women that work at these agencies have an affinity for being passionate and compassionate, and this new place was no exception.

I was cognizant that this work could be mentally and emotionally exhausting, so I was only there a few days a month to start. It felt good to be giving back again.

It was a bit of a transition to be around people after all those months of being a recluse. Being in new surroundings and sitting with new people felt like looking at a picture through water, the view was skewed and kind of wavy, but I persevered and the picture righted quickly.

I also volunteered at the Red Cross, inputting computer data and organizing files. This was familiar work from the military. It further grounded me because it felt familiar to use work skills I'd learned in the military and later as a government contractor. The Red Cross is comprised of mostly volunteers, which tells you how dedicated and caring all these individuals must be.

These two interests gave me a sense of giving back, being part of the community, and I was making friends, too. I was back in the groove of living. Each day I ensured there was something purposeful for me to do. I was taking rein of my thoughts and feelings and consciously directing myself back to God.

Then came the landmark month of July—the one year anniversary month of when things had really gone downhill. I celebrated with joyful tears and made myself a cup of coffee in gratitude to God. I'd made it through the dark tunnel and into God's infinite love. I was vigilant about safeguarding the light of our Source in me.

By the next month, it felt as though I had finally left behind the shadowy emptiness. I could think more clearly. It was during this month that I started the outline for this book. This time it felt possible, and I found myself typing on the keyboard.

I had continued my meditation and another vision revealed where this journey was taking me.

I saw myself standing before ivory steps that led to an ancient building with colossal columns. I walked up the steps into a vivid radiance of acceptance and love.

It was images such as these that nursed me along when the churning of old tapes— *What makes you think you can write a book? Who wants to read what you have to say? You're just being vain; give it up*— rang in my head. Nonetheless, I took the leap and started writing, because it felt good and I wasn't going to deny myself this pleasure.

I now had a new purpose. You know that word used to nag at me like a jagged fingernail—*Purpose: a goal or intention.* After all these years and two careers I'd very much enjoyed, here was the most important purpose of my life. This was the core that had underlined my life—to be One with God.

I went back to Texas for a short visit in September to visit with friends. While I was there I met my friend, Dana, and we went on a lunch date. When she and I first met we had an immediate spirit connection. She's the first person who recognized I was going through a spiritual crisis. She was the first person I had felt safe enough with to be vulnerable and share some of what had been happening with me. She's a wholehearted friend who saw me at my worst, and, thankfully, saw me recovered.

We met at Subway. When I saw Dana I was so happy I gave her the biggest hug, forgetting I wasn't the type to show too much affection in public. We got settled in and started talking. She was so surprised and, I think, a bit puzzled by the changes in me. We had been phoning and emailing, but Dana was not prepared for this new me. She had been expecting me to still be broken spirited. As we were eating and talking some previous clients came into the deli. I was overjoyed to see them, too. I embraced them and lovingly and enthusiastically asked how they were doing. When I sat down Dana looked at me with bewilderment. Where was her old friend who had been reserved in meeting clients outside of work?

After that, our lunch hour was devoured rather quickly, not just the food, but the time. I was literally pulsing with exuberance. There was so much I wanted to convey about what had happened since we parted; it was unusual for me to talk so much. She seemed to feast on the animation playing across my face. She hadn't expected this. The quiet, insecure friend who left in the previous year was gone.

Dana was aware of this book, which was another topic of discussion. I was excited to share my thoughts and ideas on this inspiration from God. She was excited about this message of saying "Hello, God" through others. She had never heard of such a book.

I took that as a good sign to move forward on writing about God's message that was given to me.

Our lunch came to an end. I continued on with my visit to other friends in the area. I shared about my book with other friends. They were so excited for me. They looked forward to when I would publish it. My visit came to an end and I headed back to South Carolina.

When I got back, I was still searching for a job, but the area and the economy weren't panning out. Surprisingly, I was okay about it—the lifetime fear of not having money was no longer weighing on me. That in itself has been a miracle! Thank You, God.

While I was going through the deepest part of my spiritual crisis things associated with money would almost put me in a panic. Going into a store had been challenging because thoughts about how much money everything cost would intrude and I would rush to get out; it was extremely disconcerting. So, once again, here was an occasion to say, "Hello, God," to the merchandise. Funny isn't it? But it worked.

I've discovered so many ways and places to apply greeting God. And as the saying goes: It's made all the difference.

Part II:

The Journey Back

In this time of turmoil,

May our thoughts be clear,

May our feelings be compassionate,

May our needs be fulfilled,

And may we create peace.

—Buddhist Prayer

7

It's Made All the Difference

THIS PROCESS HAS ENRICHED MANY areas of my life starting with my marriage. We already had a good relationship. But sometimes I had taken Dominic for granted. I wasn't negligent, just wasn't as appreciative as I should have been. The more I concentrated on living *"Hello, God"* I began to see how I had let minor annoyances become bigger than they merited.

This process helped me redirect my thoughts to whom and what we actually are: two people committed to each other in God. I renewed our vows in my mind. It's freeing to be vulnerable with my mate. And on top of that, he just enjoys me being me. What a gift.

During this time, Jerad's marriage went through some upheavals. Living this process has stopped me from reacting with worry. In the past I would have worried lots, and then lots more; after all, this adult man is my child. Instead, Dominic and I assured him of our unconditional love. We offered guidance, if he was amendable to it, and generally got out of the way while he sorted through his

choices. We were able to give guidance without pressure or judgment. This gave Jerad the room to do what he felt was necessary,
and made him comfortable enough to turn to us for support. Again,
this was God's guidance getting us through.

While living this process, Dominic's daughter, Kay, (who is very
loving and oh, so strong) asked if she could call me mom. Can you
fathom how honored I was by the request? It is so evident how
much she loves her father, and Kay was offering me this honor.
Words cannot express how deeply touched I was and still am by this
gift. I was also now officially nana to Kay's two daughters.

When I think of all my blessings, I see a bowl of cereal with milk
being poured over each nugget, filling each crack and cranny. It's
God's love saturating every crack and cranny of me; I feel like a little
kid listening for the snap and crackle—God is laughing with me. I
know this is a silly comparison, but it's a great visual.

God's love fills me up, literally and figuratively. I originally
viewed this process as just another tool to add to my spiritual
toolbox. But it has been a colossal surprise. If this is what it means
to have the faith of a mustard seed then I stand in miracles a lot.

The transformation is beyond anything I could have imag-
ined—the course of my life has been altered. All I knew then was
that I desperately yearned to be delivered back into Source's envel-
oping embrace. Now, my internal view of life is peaceful. Gone are
the chaotic, fearful, and absorbing egotistical thoughts. Every person I meet is God, so I'm always seeing God, talking with God. At

the forefront of my awareness is God and everyone is a joy to meet. I live in a peace and happiness in literally every area of my life.

My outside world feels significantly reshaped by God's love because I am able to view my life from a peaceful place. Yet, not that much in my world has changed on the outside. We still live in the same place; our income is basically the same. My day-to-day life is a pleasure to live. My world is created in loving, joyful appreciation, and I faithfully *savor* the moments (moments can be breathtaking,). The hiccups in life are still there, but not sidetracking me, at least not for long. God is, and I am in God.

Before I move onto the next chapter, I'd like to share an obscure passage from a book that a friend shared years ago: *"In my world nothing ever changes."* We talked about this phrase and what it meant to us. I felt it meant that I can live from peace inside myself regardless of what is happening in the world. I'm not all the way there but I'm working on it.

Jared shared a story with me that reinforced this passage. It's about a tree that dates back to 900 A.D. I thought about the myriad number of events, over the thousands of years of time, this tree had stood in observance. I ruminated over how there will always be occurrences happening in this world and that nonetheless this tree withstood them all, a tree. If I could learn to be in observance of life like that and realize that things come and go, yet God is always constant, then nothing in my world would ever change.

8

Home in God

I MADE IT HOME USING this process in 3 steps. Each "hello" built on the other, strengthening my desire to be Home. This time I wanted a foundation for my Home that would endure as I weathered the trials and treasures of living. Daily mindfulness was the brick and mortar that was constructing my Home in God.

Each offered gift of kindness, consideration, and love fused together and built a solid foundation and fortifying framework. This Home, like any other home, requires loving care and repairs. Guess what, "*Hello, God*" provided the necessary care and repair. Amazing, an all-in-one product!

My Home affords me safety and security as long as I continue to care for it. I can't tell you how many times I repeated "*Rome wasn't built in a day*" to remind myself that building my Home would take time and effort. If I wanted a life in God, I was going to have to work at it, just like anything else in life.

Just as being a loving spouse takes work, so, too, does my relationship with God. If I wanted God as my companion, I had to be willing to make this same type of investment.

This process brought a healing that I feel all the way to my soul toes, so to speak. I'm able to see God not just in others, but literally everywhere. In accepting and nurturing God's loving presence in my life—God became *real* to me, He's my Home. Although I live in this world, I understand it's just a temporary place that I experience, and I'm actually living in God all the time.

I found in focusing on God, the choices of this world were not so perplexing. God's peace and love lights the path I walk. In making God my reality, my Home, I am present in God. What a beautiful thing to be able to say.

Take a moment and savor God as your Home. Savor the feeling, the thought of how totally wonderful it feels. Now, pause and think again of God's presence in you, now in His children. Let the Infinite touch you in your mother, father, brother, sister, your children, your friends. Take a few moments or minutes to think on this.

Magnify these warm, joyful encounters and you get an idea of how it feels saying hi to God. It wakes me up! I'm in the spirit light of God's love. Think of a newborn baby, or an adorable puppy and you just have to smile at the miracle of life. Bump that smile up a hundred times over. That's what it feels like saying, "Hello, God." Every single time it awakens me into God's Infinite Allness. I am hooked, simply hooked. I'm like a baby suckling for substance, hungering for the next touch of God's love.

It's absolutely astounding! I look forward to every greeting. How can I not? This childlike wonder hasn't left me even after a year.

Some advice on pacing yourself as you make your way back Home, in case you begin questioning yourself and feeling as though experiencing God should happen quicker: Remember that introducing a new thought process takes repeated practice to learn. It takes time to install a new skill in our mind. Even if we enjoy the learning of that skill, it takes time. Practice, practice, and more practice is vital. And before you know it you will be smiling—for you are in God's light.

9

God and You

THIS JOURNEY IS ABOUT GOD and you. It's about the place where you meet God, if you're willing. This process isn't a passage to worldly riches. It is about the richness of living life peacefully.

God's peace isn't about perfection in this life. Life's ups and downs still happen to me. However, living from Source opens my mind to constructive ways of dealing with life.

I don't so often resort to my ego-self for answers. To clarify, when I reference "ego," it's the word I use for the choices I make that separate me from God. Ego choices inevitably lead to a lesson or two, probably more before it sinks in. Ego choices I've found tilts toward attempts to ensure I come out good without too much consideration for the other person.

So, no, my life isn't perfect. I still experience the burdens of living—be it children, finances, family. Only now I navigate with God at the helm. The lows are not so low and the highs are acknowledged and appreciated. More often than not peace and contentment are the treasured norm.

Let me move on—to you in particular. The use of this process will become about *your* relationship with God and not your relationship with another. This journey is truly about you! Please don't let how someone does or does not respond get in your way.

Take note of how *you feel* when applying this process. You gave God and received God simultaneously from just one greeting. There was no waiting, it happened in that very moment.

You will find in giving God you recognized God's child. From this came *recognition of yourself and the other person as children of God.* And *now* because you *recognize* this you are able to consciously give God's love and receive God's love in that instance!

Think of how happy and grateful you would feel to meet that one person you've always wanted to know, or had the chance to talk with your dearest departed loved ones. Magnify those feelings a hundredfold, that's *you* experiencing God's presence.

You and I get to orbit in God's boundless light with our spirits unrestrained. We are enfolded by a love beyond earthly understanding. It's blissfully humbling to be so treasured and loved.

As we pass on this peace and joy perhaps the next person pays the greeting forward in a smile, through a thank you, or a compliment.

You will likely touch many people's lives on this pilgrimage. I have a treasure chest of God greetings to cherish. Yet, due to the transitory nature of these greetings I seldom personally share in someone else's journey Home. Please, don't let the lack of validation affect, distract, or prevent you from continuing Home to God.

Don't take it personally. It's possible that greetings makes someone uncomfortable or not sure of what to do, or maybe they just don't like being bothered, whatever the reason, it's okay. The lack of a response is not a reflection that you aren't likable, or have somehow failed. *You succeeded.* Let me repeat: *you succeeded.*

You reached out and *you* touched God through that person. Those few seconds were all about *you* talking and seeing God in His child. You loved, shared love, and felt loved by God. Know that in your hello they felt God's love, if only for an instance, and they were moved.

This is *your* journey to God that needs *your* care and no one else can travel it for you. It's your soul you have care of and it yearns to be Home. Hopefully, along the path someone joins you, if not keep on with your journey to God's Oneness.

It's alright to be joyful! This is a good thing you did. *You* made the choice to draw and feed your soul from God's breath with a grace filled greeting. Go ahead and pat yourself on the back and give yourself a hug—God Is.

10

Other Ways to Use the Process

WHEN I STARTED ON THIS journey my thought was only about getting mentally and spiritually healthy. I had no idea how life-changing it would be. I am able to see God through others. This is worth emphasizing, *seeing* God more regularly now—every day in all men and women—has changed my view of this world. It is no longer a burden; for *God's Essence* has bejeweled my world.

I was noticing God's Essence daily in commonplace surroundings such as in a breeze of air, crickets calling, or squirrels running up a tree. God over and over was there before me. I laughed out loud—there was God.

There were also times when it just wasn't possible to offer a direct, "Hello, God." For example: driving, working, at the movies, watching TV, in a crowd, or perhaps in a place that doesn't seem safe (you get the idea). The premise remains the same, however, to acknowledge God in others and yourself.

I do this while I'm driving. I must look pretty silly with a smile plastered on my face. In busy traffic God greetings slow down my rush-rush feelings. It's pretty hard to get too upset when thinking with God.

One day I was waiting for an opening to turn right at an intersection (from the only right-hand lane), and another car squeezed in. The driver startled me; we could have caused an accident. This was a real chance to employ the *"Hello, God"* attitude. Yep, this process can be a labor of love.

In work settings, I can come across as brisk and abrupt if there are project deadlines. This process redirects me and I remember to smile, slowdown, and even take a break.

It's absolutely great in crowds like restaurants, strolling through the mall, or out shopping. I'm in the awareness of God, over and over. It's a natural high. Hard to believe I could go into a crowded place before and just sit, read a book, and not pay attention to anyone.

When my son was in high school I chaperoned a pizza party. Jerad's teacher was looking forward to meeting me; she thought I'd be as outgoing as he was. Jerad told her, not my mom; she'll probably bring a book and go read. That is exactly what I did.

I used to avoid dealing with people in places of business. That's all changed. I recall an associate at an automotive store who had a boot brace on his right foot. I commented about how it must be difficult to stand all day. He shared how it happened and we ended up talking a bit. Also, on the plus, plus side, I get better service now that I live with this new attitude. Anyhow, since we are wired to share, why not share God in each exchange.

Going into a store use to be a quick get in and get out, dodging any situation where I might need to speak with anyone. Not now! I walk in spritely, my hair swinging, and naturally smiling.

This also works with business calls. I make a point to remember the associate's name; after all, I'm talking to God's child. By keeping this thought in mind, I'm willing to work with them.

Being kind and courteous to God's child tends to help me get things resolved more efficiently with cooperation and friendliness. I'll usually ask if I can leave a positive comment with their supervisor. Our connection was in God and everyone benefited.

You can even use this process watching TV or movies. Hey, no one has to know about your "Hello, God" to the screen. The people on the screen are still real people. Then there's also social networking. It's a great resource to extend God to others. I try to only share uplifting, positive, or funny comments.

At home I'll just go around saying, "Hello, God." Upon awaking, I say, "Good morning, God" to welcome in the new day. One of the best ones: "Have a God day."

I've already spoken about greeting God through nature. Sometimes I think it's easier for many of us to see God's hand in nature versus mankind.

My family has its own personal angel, who, without realizing, showed me what God's unconditional love looks like. I made a promise to live love just as she did. Starting off conversations with God in mind reminds me to listen and be there in the moment for my loved ones. With God, I'm more relaxed and feel less compelled to fix things. In effect, I'm hearing God and that means there's no need for judgments. Do I always succeed? No. But, mine is a life-long *"Hello, God"* vocation.

Then there are my friends. Our connections have deepened because I'm willing to be genuinely vulnerable, honest, and share at deeper levels. I can relax and chillax (my attempt at being hip here). It's liberating not to have to have the answers. I'm willing to be defenseless, trusting God as my guide.

One of the most unforeseen ways to say hello to God looks me in the mirror every day: myself. Honestly, I'm the last person I thought to say this to, how bewildering is that? I'd said God is in me, but had not looked at myself and said the words, "Hi, God. You are in me!" I just stood there beaming as Source's light filtered through my spirit. I was mesmerized by the reflection of God looking back at me. I walked away amusingly laughing at me and God in the mirror.

God and me; it sounds so good.

Part III:

Not Their Journey

People are often unreasonable, irrational, and self-centered. Forgive them anyway.

If you are kind, people may accuse you of selfish, ulterior motives. Be kind anyway.

If you find serenity and happiness, some may be jealous.

Be happy anyway.

The good you do today, will often be forgotten.

Do good anyway.

Give the best you have, and it will never be enough.

Give your best anyway.

In the final analysis, it is between you and God.

It was never between you and them anyway.

—Mother Teresa

11

How Did Seeing God Happen?

MAYBE YOU'RE WONDERING, HOW WAS she able to see God in others? Is it really possible to focus on God in others, *see* God? It may sound like an over-generalization—just focus on God. But, is it possible? Yep, it is. This process in 3 steps ended up being the key that opened the celestial door to this simple, yet ponderous question.

Throughout this journey I questioned and bumped into areas of my life that needed to change. I acknowledge those areas that needed change and then started doing something about them; it felt like doing a good spring cleaning.

Previous to pioneering down this new path, I honestly considered myself to be a fairly nice person who worked at being positive and kind. I wish I could tell you I always made allowances for someone being different from me, but that wouldn't be the truth. It wasn't as easy as one, two, three—setting aside difference and accepting others.

Even though I'd professed to believe God was in everyone, I did not unwaveringly hold this belief. My impressions got in the way, and from there I would then decide how to respond/react to someone.

Another area that surfaced dealt with my overly healthy respect for authority, due to a father who was a bit of a disciplinarian, and then to the military life I led for over twenty years. This insight showed me that it was okay to let this go.

I also had a habit of fretting about family and friends. I just knew it was my responsibility to have *the* answers. I didn't even begin to realize how quickly I took on someone else's problems. No one asked me to; I just did it. I'm not blaming anyone. It was me. Thankfully, I developed responsible boundaries and learned to help without *owning* their problems.

And, oh, yeah—that money issue! I didn't understand and was afraid to understand. I had no game plan on how to handle money. I view and spend money with trust now. It's no longer the Big Bad Boogey Man because God is at the helm. Money is no longer bigger than God—a very important understanding for me.

What I'm alluding to is that I got out of my way, and let God lead.

This process challenged me to question how I lived my story, my view of others, and resulted in really knowing and living a God life of peace and offering it to others.

This brings me back to the question I asked at the start of this chapter: *Is it possible to focus on God?* I say again, yes, it is! As you start re-directing your focus you will gradually begin seeing God in others. It will take time. Changing any thought process takes time. Shifting my focus has allowed me to see the *Greatness of God in each of us.*

Think on this story. A Lakota child asked his grandfather, "Grandfather, which is more important to love or be loved?" Grandfather replied, "Which is more important to the bird, the left wing or the right wing?

Obviously the answer is neither. We are all equally important. We all want to be loved, but the hard part is to love. I see God because I look with God's love. We are brilliant splendors of Infinite's magnificence displayed here on earth.

God's love truly exceeds human understanding.

12

Embrace God in Your Story

UP TO NOW I'VE EMPHASIZED ways of not getting caught up in another person's story. There's another side to be considered— experiencing God in your own story. Just as the person you greet has a story, so, too, do you. The story of your life is still with you; you've lived it every day of your life. I'm not asking you to discount your life story in working this process. What I'm suggesting is you expand past your story and embrace God in you.

I realized that embracing God (instead of my story) required changing the video recorder in my mind. This recorder was automatically *reading* others. It took note of what people looked like, how they sounded, what their tone conveyed, what they were wearing, etcetera. It made assumptions about observations and interpreted people's personalities. It's amazing how what is recorded plays under the surface of our conscious awareness.

My recorder needed to be reset. As I sat writing in the café, I decided to try an experiment. Here's what I did. I went to the mall and started observing people. I looked at people walking by and started saying hi. I noticed that I got impressions that some people were: quiet, loud, courteous, rude, outgoing, shy, lonely, loving, intolerant, colorful, sad, happy…. What do you think you might notice? It's curiously remarkable what we take in without realizing it. We just automatically take it in.

I wondered at why I subconsciously got impressions about people? What came to mind was that I used these stored recordings as a way to experience myself through reflections of similarities or differences between others and myself. This automatic and ongoing "record" of events let me know if I was safe or not.

In re-directing what I recorded about others, I noticed an increased ability to stand in observance of living this life. Visualize a maze and see yourself wandering down the corridors, puzzling over which turns will get you to the end. It can be fun, but it can be a mystery or a scary undertaking to be maneuvering around, attempting to make the correct turns to get to the end. It all depends on how you feel about the maze. I personally didn't know how to enjoy the adventure; I was always concerned with reaching the end.

Reaching the end for me is not so significant anymore, nor is puzzling out the maze of life. Rather, my perspective veers to viewing the maze of life from above. It's as though I'm observing from a bird's eye view. The distinction from being in the maze to watching from above allows me to just about forecast whether the words or actions being taken will achieve a desired outcome.

I hear myself saying this and it sounds pretty arrogant. It's not meant to imply I'm now a soothsayer. This type of observation allows me to be *objective*, which the Merriam Webster Dictionary defines as: *expressing or dealing with facts or conditions as perceived without distortion by personal feelings, prejudices, or interpretations.*

This has enabled me to detach from my own story. This detachment from another's personal journey and my own has released me from getting caught up (or lost in) the maze of living. I've reset my internal recorder. This objectivity is not cold. I know living this life can be hard. It's actually increased my compassion. This objectivity lets me know that it's going to be okay no matter what path is taken, for I know what meets you and me on the other side—God. This keeps me centered in living with God, instead of the world. I'm not denying this world; it's just that God has become more real.

This permitted me to switch parts in the play of my life. Instead of being the actor caught up in my role, I'm more like the director observing the scenes.

Addressing my environment from this detached standpoint makes it easier for me to feel, experience, and care without all the clutter from the story of my life.

I feel and experience, through others and myself, God in ways that I previously thought of as a far-fetched fantasy.

13

Experiences in God

EACH DAY I HAVE WONDERFUL experiences in God. As you go about your journey, you will experience equally wonderful but unique experiences, too.

One particular incident stands out. I remember shopping and a lovely woman reached out with a warm, "How are you today?" She actually took the time to acknowledge me and wait for my reply. It makes me smile just to think of it. I happily returned, "Great. Thank you, and you?" She left a vivid impression on me. I'd like to think her soul recognized my extended, "Hello, God." Through this wonderful woman, I felt I had sensed God's happiness and love of me, of us.

Another day while walking across a parking lot I passed a middle-aged man and offered a God-felt hello. His eyes registered surprised and wonder that a stranger would take the time to greet him with such open cheerfulness; he, in turn, gave me a wonderful, "How are you?" It was a brief, yet, authentic exchange.

One challenging experience gave Dominic and me an opportunity to see just how well we were applying the process. We needed some work done to our home and had hired laborers that charged by the hour. They were so slow, but there was no way we could replace them in a timely manner.

This could have been extremely frustrating for us. Instead we conceded, yes, the situation left a lot to be desired. But, and here's the key: we said these workers are God's children and had a right to be treated as such.

Did it mean we consented to their behavior? No, but getting frustrated wouldn't have changed the situation. We took it, instead, as a lesson in seeing God in a difficult situation.

I've also run across some of God's children who seem lost in their own lives. They looked lost, meek, scared, withdrawn. They seemed to have forgotten they are a child of the Universal Being. I can personally relate to these types of feelings. There were times when I found it hard to believe anyone cared for me, never mind feeling like one of God's children. When someone offered a simple greeting it lifted my heart.

There was a young man who worked at the café where I wrote most of this book. He was always quiet and looked a little unsure. He seemed to take pride in keeping the sitting area clean. I thanked him for his efforts and asked his name. It turned out he had health difficulties and was thankful that his work was appreciated. After our exchange, he seemed to stand taller, with an inner glow.

One day when picking up the mail I noticed the lobby was unusually full. Previously, I would have turned around and come back another time; instead I walked right in. The people in front of me were what could be called loud. In back of them were a couple of others who were exchanging jail-time stories. Off to the side was a reserved, well-heeled, smartly dressed lady. Then there was an older gent who looked like life had taken a toll, but he had survived with grace. There was also another young man who just looked bored. Divinely, due to God, my thoughts as I walked in the door were—here are God's children regardless of my impressions. I sent a soundless encircling "Hello, God" to all, next I said hello to each person, and every single person said hi right back to me.

I've developed a habit when shopping of taking note of an associate's name, or note of any badges on their vests. Most people like sharing what each badge means and what it took to earn it. Source gets the credit for bringing me to this mindset. I would never have been able to do this on my own.

In good conscience I can say that when I bring God to my greetings, I feel contented and happy 100% of the time. This may sound like I'm stretching the truth, I'm not—100% of the time I feel this way when I see God in others.

14

God's Essence

IT TOOK TIME FOR ME to truly see the inner glow of God's Essence in others. I feel that Infinite's Essence is the star dust that we all originated from. It matters not what we do or don't do—Infinite's Essence cannot be destroyed. But, we can forget as we get spellbound living our day-to-day life. We can become magnetized into thinking we are our story, or by getting caught up in someone else's life story.

Recognition of Infinite's Essence is akin to a child's slate of innocent love that has yet not been overwritten. I recognize that Essence is always present, whether God's child comes from a loving foundation or lacks one. Essence recognized can become a seedling that brings forth a bounty or it can wither from neglect on barren soil.

It's this Essence that beckons me to continue on with my journey. Is it a wonder I live in beauty? Honoring Essence delivers me to trusting that there's a reason for my existence here in this world.

Sagely feeding the Essence of our souls reaps peace of mind, this is the bounty of a life lived in God. The story of my birth, childhood, and adulthood can become all that I know of myself, or I can stay cognizant of God's Essence and live from there. It's a choice I make every single day because I am only too fragilely human.

I've discovered that every greeting awakens Source's Essence in me. Each day I make a choice to draw from Source's Essence to grace my life or draw from my ego. Ego only complicates my life and adds more lessons to be learned.

My ego labors to extinguish this Essence and take me back to relying on my judgments. This is what eventually took me down the rabbit hole. When I err again, because I'm still learning, another lesson waits in the wings. The magnificence of God is that it doesn't matter. I'm always Home.

This realization was an insight into the depth of God's divineness. It's hard to put into words the magnitude of how unconditionally we are all of God. We are as stars dotting God's universe.

15

God or Ego

I CAN WALK IN THE space of God's love, or choose to let my ego lead the way. Let me restate what I mean by ego—it's what separates me from God, and tilts toward ensuring I come out good without too much consideration for others.

In choosing the first, receiving God's child, I know moments of being in Source's presence.

On the flip side, I've walked way too often with my ego leading, looking for ways to feel superior, smarter, wiser…or neglected, victimized, put down.

I have been the person who thought and acted as though I was so much better than someone else, as though they weren't worthy of my time, let alone a simple greeting. This, of course, meant there was going to be a price to be paid.

All the times I chose ego only lengthened the time it took to learn the lesson, to dust myself off and get back up. Looking back, I have to honestly admit my seemed *better-ness* was pretty shallow.

But the one feeling I never felt when I chose from my ego was—peace. Let me demonstrate with a horizontal graph.

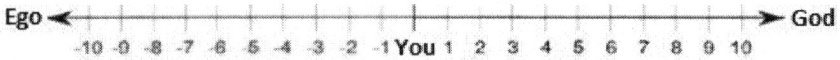

Ego ⟵———————————————————⟶ God
-10 -9 -8 -7 -6 -5 -4 -3 -2 -1 You 1 2 3 4 5 6 7 8 9 10

You are at the center. Look at the graph and envision each God greeting creating a notch to the right, moving you closer to God. Making the choice to inch your way to God will eventually lead you Home and the ego will become a distant echo. But, conversely each ego choice creates a notch to the left leading to new lessons. Something to think about....

The choice became increasingly obvious: choose God, it works. Hitting my head against my battered-up ego wall hurt, literally and figuratively. What felt like a need spurred on by ego, could only be satiated by getting my way. Yet, I did not get the approval or satisfaction I ultimately sought. This fleeting stroke never brought me what I was yearning for—peace of mind in God, love.

This simple process brought me face-to-face with myself and sometimes what I saw wasn't pretty. The biggest and most important act to get past my ego **was to admit to my own shortcomings**.

When I looked back there was a trail littered with the many faces my ego wore: pridefulness, arrogance, and vanity to name a few.

Pride wouldn't let me reach out for help, vanity wouldn't let me admit I needed help, and arrogance made me think I could do it all by myself. These were the band aids I'd relied on to make it through life, and none had healed me.

Getting past ego choices continues to be one of the most difficult feats of this journey. But, you know what? Admitting my shortcomings has freed me. Being defenseless hasn't been that scary. Those months of despair laid bare my vulnerabilities. They lost their strength, deflating flat like a hot air balloon—pretenses filled with hot air that seeped away when I faced the light of God. I had made my fears larger than life, larger than God.

I don't have to wear so many different faces to deal with people or life. Facing my own faults shifted power away from my ego. Isn't it confounding that using this simple process left me both defenseless and protected before God?

My fear of saying hi wasn't huge, but it had been persistent. The seed that had sown this came from the fear of taking the initiative. In my tangled thoughts I needed permission before acting on my own. Looking back through my storyline, it became evident I often waited for permission to do things. Without it, I felt I would get in trouble. And when I did take the initiative, I'd feel guilty. When I finally questioned the guilt, I realized it was just an old habit that was holding sway over me.

This insight revealed other strings that were attached to this habit. There was the possibility of rejection or hurt feelings if I didn't get permission (something to be avoided at all costs). There was also the need to impress others and this led to worldly comparisons. I used to feel that failure, true or perceived, was something I had to be protected from at all costs. I had to feel that I was successful! So much better to be rewarded or recognized, was isn't? Those vulnerabilities said to me that I was supposed to be more than whatever I asked of myself, or what someone else wanted of me.

Now that God is real they've evaporated like a mist when the sun shines through. I've accepted them as emotions I go through, but no longer permit them to cling to me. What's left to defend?

Thankfully, with vigilance, ego more often rides in the backseat. This book was made possible because of God's loving guidance, not by my ego.

There is an old Indian story that conveys the message of choosing between God and ego.

An old chief was teaching his grandson about life. "A fight is going on inside me," he said to the boy. "It is a terrible fight and it is between two wolves. One is bad—he is anger, envy, sorrow, regret, greed, arrogance, self-pity, guilt, resentment, inferiority, lies, false pride, superiority, self-doubt, and ego.

"The other is good—he is joy, peace, love, hope, serenity, humility, kindness, benevolence, empathy, generosity, truth, compassion, and faith. This same fight is going on inside you and inside every other person, too."

The grandson thought about it for a minute and then asked his grandfather, "Which wolf will win?"

The old chief simply replied, "The one you feed."

The choice to feed the good wolf takes me to God where there is peace beyond human understanding. I can see myself on the mountain top with God, the bird's eye view, and it's beautiful.

Part IV:

Healing

"Lord, make me an instrument of thy peace.

Where there is hatred, let me sow love;

Where there is injury, pardon;

Where there is doubt, faith;

Where there is despair, hope;

Where there is darkness, light;

Where there is sadness, joy.

O divine Master, grant that I may not so much seek

To be consoled as to console,

To be understood as to understand,

To be loved as to love.

For it is in giving that we receive;

It is in pardoning that we are pardoned…"

—Francis of Assisi

16

The Changes, the Healing

WHAT WAS I LIKE BEFORE God whispered to me? Friends had described me as reserved and cautious, sometimes hesitant, a good listener, kind, observant, confident, but distant. Now they describe me as being extraverted, which implies friendly and outgoing. I'm still a good listener, work at being God kind, and, as always, observant. Am I healed? Mostly.

I call myself a child of the Almighty and experience contentment, joy, laughter, smiles, and peace.

Claiming my heritage permitted me to see this world with a pristine clarity instead of through the confusing maze in my mind. Why had I kept missing the mark? Clarity showed me how silly I had been for trying to do it on my own. Sure, I'd asked God for help, I'd get help, and then think I'm all grownup and that I could do it on my own. Sound familiar? Just like a kid I'd be in a rush. Surrendering drew back the curtains that had cloaked my rightful inheritance—God's treasure chest of love. I am one of those treasures. There is no lack in me. I am enough.

I'd been treading the waters of life until coming back to my ultimate purpose—to make my way back to God. This pursuit of Oneness has filtered throughout my life. Hopefully, this time I won't stray back into absorption of day-to-day life, or spiritual arrogance and smugness.

What is it about this fervent pressure of having a purpose in this life? This need drives us to reach for something; but we're not always clear on what it is; or we're left feeling like it's out of reach; or that we have somehow failed.

For me it meant needing a reason to get up each day. I have to do something while I'm living this life. I have to have something to look forward to, otherwise the days are empty. I don't think a life purpose has to have some magical intent. I say this because I've heard people ask, "Just what is my purpose in life?" The answer doesn't have to be specific.

What if, as an alternative, we purposely took care of *each moment?* What would we find if we lived each moment, instead of living in yesterday or tomorrow? Might we find our Higher Power and hear wisdom that could guide us to life with a purpose? Yes, I believe so.

I choose as my purpose to be closer to my Higher Power. The thoughts I act on between birth and death can bring me closer to my Higher Power. This is the purpose I can give to a day, a relationship, or a job. A wonderful friend shared with me about a very old minister she knew whose purpose every day was walking with God; in each gesture, word, and deed. Isn't that beautiful?

For those of you who have found your particular purpose(s), count yourself blessed and bring your Higher Power to that purpose and watch how your passion grows. For those still searching, why not bring Source to each moment and perhaps you will find what you've been searching for. We are only here a short while, and though life can be tiresome, it can also be beautiful.

I've also observed how purpose can get confused with pride. We get so prideful of what we do and how we see ourselves. Look up the word pride. There are not many favorable definitions. It was pride that got the better of me when I was a peer counselor. I didn't reach out soon enough for help, and pride was part of my downfall.

There's a saying that fits here: *"Pride starts in heaven, falls to earth, and ends in hell."* It finally makes sense to me.

Pride starts in heaven—since we come from God.

Falls to earth—our ego takes over and it becomes about, "Look at what I've achieved!" Or in the opposite direction, like when we tell ourselves we should be more.

Ends in hell—delivered to hell because we got lost in this world, absorbed by our circumstances.

There is a way out of this cycle. I'm convinced that my life purpose, no matter how many times I get off-track, is being in Oneness with God, in this Always Moment. Each time I stray this is the answer that rescues me.

I mentioned spiritual arrogance and smugness before my crisis. I had become prideful, arrogant, and smug about having achieved

God's peace. I was taking credit for this God-given accomplishment. While speaking with friends who were also on a spiritual journey there were times when instead of offering compassion, understanding, and withholding judgment, I was cavalier. That was the epitome of spiritual arrogance. Is it any wonder I had a downward slide?

This crisis taught me how easy it is to fall. God may have had my back, but my back was turned. It's not possible to be arrogant when God is guiding the ship. Envision standing before the Supreme Source—magnificence that is All Power, All Love. Only humility is possible before this Greatness. I had no business taking credit for something that I humanly couldn't do. This is why peace is beyond human understanding—because it's of God. It was only through the grace of God that peace came to me before, and it is only through that same grace that I live in God's peace today.

Writing this book has been healing. I've been able to ponder and share how this process has unfolded. Writing about this process has helped me to stay on track. It has centered me, humbled me before God.

There were other changes that are more readily apparent to the eye. It's become effortless to speak with others. I enjoy sharing and taking the time to learn about Gods' children. Previously talking or being around others used to be draining—today, not so much.

I also clued into the genesis of my need to take care of just about everyone, as well as the reason for being introverted. I had been a child with a lot of responsibilities. Responsibility, I thought, meant

I had to be the one with the answers, which my little child mind interpreted as being the one that had to listen and react. The little girl in me thought this meant that others' needs were more important than my own. What an insight! And a relief to let go of—the *need* to have to.

It's not such a big deal anymore. Time with family and friends doesn't mean pressure to care for everyone anymore. Instead, I find myself chuckling, laughing, sharing, and just being silly. My story is not so heavy anymore. Living from this space there are moments when my gratitude and love of God washes over and overwhelms me; then the moment becomes still, bringing me close to tears. God is the Significant in my life and my story became my vehicle back to God.

The overriding trait that kept me from changing my life was being afraid to take the initiative. This fear, I'm glad to say, has been smashed to smithereens! I just tell myself, "Go for it, get over it and do something." God's company gave me the courage to reach inside and take action—this book was one of those "actions."

I used to come up with all kinds of excuses not to take the initiative like: *I'm too scared. I'll get in trouble. What if it doesn't work?* Visualize a junkyard with heaps of garbage, that's what my lack of courage looked like. Talk about waste. With that visual in mind, imagine just how ginormous a light bulb moment this was for me.

I recalled reading about near-death experiences where people reported that during the crossover one of the first things that happened was a life review. The life review wasn't a composite of scenes from their viewpoint, but from the *perspective of how others* experienced encounters with them. That really got my attention.

I recalled wondering what kind of life review I would have, and questioned what others must have experienced because of my actions or words. Some of it would be good, but there would be some really not so good times. This insight prompted me to start doing daily reviews.

Every day I mindfully project through my deeds, words, thoughts, and body language what I would like another to take from their encounter with me. It has become a habit to automatically catalog my day. I must admit it's a good feeling to know I've been kind to others each day.

This is another reason my personal relationships have improved. I work at them with a more giving and understanding heart. Personal relationships are the true test of this daily review; these areas are where it is easiest to slip back into old patterns.

I'd like to think my life review when I crossover (from this point on) will be one of giving, and that other's encounters with me will reflect back acceptance and appreciation. I'm kind of looking forward to it.

My husband has a name for me: The Quiet Extrovert. The extrovert—reaching out, and the quiet—being comfortable when someone shares their story. I like to think others can sense when someone is receptive to hearing about their inner-self. I want to be worthy of this privilege.

Living *"Hello, God"* settles me into Source, and it's changed the way I experience the world. I feel appreciation and thankfulness for experiencing God through this world, rather than dwelling on perceived lacks in my life.

This unfolding has manifested into a better-lived life. In order to arrive here, I'm the one who had to change. Just as a caterpillar must go into the cocoon before it emerges as the exquisite butterfly, change couldn't happen in my life until I was willing to take steps in a new direction. I re-emerged as God's child. And as fairy tales are wont to say—it's made all the difference.

17

Vision of Before and After "Hello, God."

GOD GRACED ME WITH ANOTHER rolling cinematic vision, several months into my journey, while walking Dino one day. This vision made clear to me where I had been before and after "Hello, God."

I saw myself struggling down the center of a narrow path. On either side were dense, dark towering trees that obscured the light. The forest undergrowth was packed with rocks, thick grass, leaves, and needles. My path forward was almost impossible to see through.

Each of my anxieties, uncertainties, fears, and doubts crowded in on me as I fought my way through to find some sort of clearing. I kept falling down, scraping my hands and clothing on the dense trees and foliage. I felt claustrophobic as I made my way through the wildwoods that seemed to be clutching back at me. My heart was pounding so hard I could hear it echoing in my ears.

I labored to stay on this narrow rock-pitted path. I could hear myself pleading for a way out. I was flailing and thrashing my arms; pushing aside elongated thick-coiled vines of anxieties and doubts, and breathing hard from all the exertion.

Thank God, I saw pinpoint flashes in the dim shadows. I felt that if I could just reach the light I'd make my way out from my fears that were encroaching me.

Finally, I emerged onto a four-foot ledge of rock-packed ground. Behind me was the dense forest of dreads. I looked back at the path I had struggled through. It was almost swallowed up. I walked to the edge and saw a deep gorge at least twenty feet wide. It looked bottomless. As I looked across, I saw a dense mist-shrouded field. If I could just get to the other side of the gorge, there was hope that all my pain and struggle would finally be over.

But, how was I to get to the other side? There was no bridge! How? I closed my eyes thinking there had to be a way. I couldn't have been brought this far and not be given a way to reach the other side. There just had to be a way. When I opened my eyes I saw each "Hello, God" weaving together a sturdy hemp rope bridge, with slim wooden boards to walk across. Each greeting strengthened, thickened, and lengthened the bridge.

I watched in wonder as this bridge stretched securely across the gorge. I tentatively started crossing, taking cautious steps because I didn't want to look down into the chasm, I might falter into the obscurity that I had struggled to outmaneuver. I kept walking across with my gaze on the dense mist. As I made my way nearer, the mist thinned and within it was a glowing light. Before I knew it I'd reached the other side. I'd made it!

There I was on solid ground thanking God over and over. After catching my breath, I noticed the mist had dissolved completely, and before me were two immense, ancient-looking wooden doors with no handles. They were impressive in their grandeur, mahogany and thick, meeting in an arch on the top. I didn't feel nervous or afraid, and so I walked up to the doors and lightly touched them, kind of testing to see how they opened. Like magic, they glided apart to a welcoming space of shimmering whiteness.

I stepped into the luminescent whiteness and immediately felt totally secure. I'd stepped into God's unconditional love that enfolded and saturated my being. I sensed the loving vague silhouettes of family that had passed on over the years. In particular, I sensed the presence of my favorite grandmother, who I'd always felt so loved by. I sensed the resounding love and guidance from, not only her, but also other departed loved ones. As I looked around, I started crying. I felt my dad's acceptance and joyful delight and love. Then all of sudden, I was back in the present and unconscious tears were rolling down my cheeks. I was in awe.

At that moment, I was One with God who had never left me, had held me through it all, and brought me back to Source's embrace. I was as free as a small child spinning in circles, getting giddy and dizzy in innocent bliss.

What an amazing experience. I can't live there all the time be-cause there is everyday life to be lived, but I hold this vision and know that whatever happens, everything will be okay.

18

God's Power

THERE IS SO MUCH UNTAPPED power in this "Hello, God" greeting. Can you imagine the collective power of goodwill that could come from giving and living this simple pleasantry? The pooled positive energy of everyone saying hello to God could generate rippling waves of goodwill, creating a whole lot more happy people. Just envision it.

In the past I doubted my ability to affect others, let alone the world. Today I'm conscious of impacting lives just by existing.

We, you and me, make a change in this world every, single day—we touch the lives of those we know or encounter just by going through our day. Remember the butterfly effect or how throwing a rock into water creates a ripple? You and I create ripples in this life. There is not one of us who doesn't, because we each have an impact on our environment.

You are not inconsequential; you have worth. Recognize what a power you are individually…and we are collectively. Don't give your power away.

There was a Native American who left his tribe to live in American society. He became so absorbed in living his new life that he lost his way. He had given over his power to others, and his life then had many trials. He finally returned back to the reservation to find answers. It took time, for he had forgotten how to live in his spirit. He finally recalled his spirit power and was healed of his ailments and confusion.

I had done this, given away my God power to others, to the world, to everyone but me. I hadn't trusted myself. I was drinking from the world, thinking I would find the answers there. It was when I returned to the river of my soul that peace came. I came to understand that to expect more from someone than what is there, just disappoints me. It zaps me and belittles my God-given power.

This power released me from the hurt, anger, grudges, and judgments I'd held onto for years (for someone I had dearly loved in this life). These hurts had held sway over me, so much that I couldn't see him clearly. Even though I was an adult, I had been seeing through my child's eyes. And they had been clouded with confusion. The child didn't have the capacity to see how life affects us, and how unprepared we can be to deal with its curveballs. This man lives in so much of who I am, and now I love him without the cloud of hurts. Without the holes of hurt in my soul. I'm healed and whole. I forgave God's child and then I forgave myself.

That is the power of God's love at work.

Through the power of this process, I came to understand that I had been giving power to my fears. I took back my power and put it back where it belonged—with God.

God had given me this power. And I had used it unwisely. I am part of God's power. I may pull away, but I can't be separated from it. This may sound blasphemous. But, please stop and think. We are of God, then it follows we are of God's power.

We have so much *power*. We can't even begin to realize it. We may think this power is separate from us, but when we do this, we separate ourselves from God.

I wasn't "awake" enough before my *"Hello, God"* experience to see that I had given this power over to others, because I didn't trust myself. I had given my Godly power to the world in search of solace and love. I had squandered it in my yearning to be a part of something. I think most of us do this, wanting to be it part of a family, group, gang, relationship, work place, community. We search for ways to belong, but what we are actually longing for is to be back in God's Presence.

We long to belong. It's our nature to want to be a part of something. It's ingrained in us. I no longer believe the world can give you or me the solace and love that will make us feel safe and secure. Only the Original Giver can do this: God. I'd come full circle. I was Home now.

19

Inspirations from 3 Steps

LIVING THIS PROCESS HAS BEEN a labor of love and, as with most things, has taken persistent resolution. I had to get out of my own way to experience God. And in experiencing God, I know now that I am loved and cared for. Isn't that the crux of what most of us long for, to know without question that we are cared for, that we are loved and loveable? I found acceptance, rest, relaxation, joy, happiness, and unconditional love for I am Alive in the Mind of Love.

I used to struggle with my will versus God's. I came to understand that God's Will wants happiness and love for His children. The faiths I'd studied had clouded that understanding for me. I used to think that surrendering to God would leave me with a life of even more struggles. Yet, in saying yes to God's Will—that place in the center of my chest where a huge thumb was pushing down on—felt relief. Peace.

Just as one values the work that goes into owning a house, I value the daily *"Hello, God"* mindset that brought me Home to

Source. I realized that moving into a house and making it mine takes time, and so will moving into my Everlasting Home. I don't know the final move-in date; however, I do know that as long as I nurture my spirit the way will be shown to me.

Can you imagine what abiding in God's Mind would be like? Each aspect of life is brimming with God's love. This doesn't mean every single thing I've ever wanted all of sudden materializes. Actually, all the things I thought were so important before seem less and less necessary. That's freeing in itself. This has been an odd revelation (because I really thought I needed all those things).

It's when I leave God's love that my fears and supposed needs attempt to worm their way back in. However, when I dwell in God's love, not one part of me has doubts or fears because I know unconditional love.

As I meditated on this insight I was presented with the following image. I saw a squared- sized piece of paper. A large circle filled the page touching all four sides. Inside this circle was a very small circle. Inside the small circle was a dot. That dot is me; the smaller circle is the world; and the large circle is God. Ah, here is my choice—to draw from the world as my source, or God.

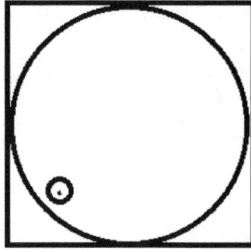

When I draw from God, I feel loving peace and happiness gently flowing into to me. I am replenished and quenched by God. Can you imagine what this feels like?

I alluded earlier to standing back and observing. Try this out. Think of watching someone; notice their actions; think of what you believe will happen in that person's life because of what they set in motion. I've worked to be able to stand back and watch myself in this same way.

What are the ripple effects I will experience because of my actions?

The more I stand back from myself and live in God, my life events tend to hold less substantial weight. "Stuff" I'd previously held as necessary for true happiness lost most of its significance. Not to say I don't or wouldn't like to have a beautiful house or take an extended vacation, it just no longer grips me like a vise. I'm not in lack; I'm in God.

Pretty weighty stuff. Once again, with time and application, choosing to live a peaceful life becomes simplified and the journey becomes smoother. This does not mean life will be perfect. But with God, it's just a bit easier.

An interesting observation: When I'm perplexing over what is in front of me (key word "perplexing"), I feel the front part of my brain working. Conversely, when I'm in what I term "my God Mind" I feel myself thinking from the crown (top) of my head.

Now that I'm aware of this, it's a good check to keep me centered on God. It keys me back in and helps me avoid getting bogged down. When I think with God on something, the solutions are more direct and effective, allowing me to let go and feel God's peace.

20

Dream Guidance

THROUGHOUT MY LIFE I'VE ASKED for spiritual guidance. The wisdom of this guidance has led me to answers on how to make peace with issues in my life. A few years ago I had a dream that changed my perception of things, and has grounded me further in a place of peace.

I was a sensitive little kid who felt things deeply. My father had a big personality. When he was in the room he was the center of attention. His approval was important to all us kids. This dream was a gift from my father, after his passing, on how to be happy.

"Happiness just for happiness's sake" had been foreign to me most of my life. This was a dream within a dream, and was in full-blown color. I saw my father, who passed at the age of fifty-nine, standing barefoot, dressed in an all-white Mexican peasant top and bottoms. He looked so young, about thirty-three, standing by a cart tethered to a short grey-colored donkey. He looked directly at me. Reflected in his eyes was all the love he had for me, and my heart swelled with joy. Then he waved his right arm out and the dream shifted to a scene from my childhood.

I was about ten. I saw myself walking happily into the kitchen saying, "Good morning." My father's back was to me as he sat at the kitchen table. He glanced back noticing a bounce in my step and said over his shoulder, "What do you have to be happy about?"

I popped awake with gratefulness in seeing this moment clearly through my dream within a dream. This was an *aha* moment. From that one, innocent question my child mind took that to mean there had to be a reason to be happy. This was why my happiness had been such an elusive bugger.

My father chose this scene so I'd know it was okay to be happy just because. Well, I had squandered knowing happiness for happiness's sake due to my earlier spiritual arrogance. But through *"Hello, God"* I found my way back, and I'm happy again—just because.

I've come to the conclusion of this book but by no means the end of the journey. My stays in God are no longer moments; they're hours long. I'm still working on fulltime, but I love the journey and the continual healing.

Thank you for sharing in this amazing adventure with me. Thank you for letting me be a part of your world, for loving me, for letting me share *"Hello, God."*

You are Loved.

A Note to the Reader

Thank you so much for reading my story. If you could take a moment to review "Hello, God." on Amazon, I would really appreciate it. Your input is important to me. God's message changed my life; I hope this for you. I would love to know how my book has impacted your life, and I'd like to grow as a writer, too. Thank you!

About the Author's Dog

Dino, my forever baby, was instrumental in helping say "Hello, God" to others. The first few months of my journey Dino was with me on my daily walks. His presence and naturally friendly demeanor made it easier to reach out. People wanted to say "hi" back when they saw Dino. I truly thank God for Dino every day. He has been with me for seven wonderful years now.

God's Day to all.

Acknowledgements

Many thanks to my editor, Lisa Cerasoli. Her guidance helped me find the voice to write this message. This book would not have been possible without her.

To my husband, Dominic—for encouraging me to pursue my dream.

"Hello, God."
A PROCESS IN 3 STEPS

Made in the USA
Middletown, DE
18 November 2016